AMERICA TODAY

From a Christian's Point of View

Louis "Lou" Salamone

WESTBOW
PRESS®
A DIVISION OF THOMAS NELSON
& ZONDERVAN

WestBow Press books may be ordered through booksellers or by contacting:

WestBow Press
A Division of Thomas Nelson & Zondervan
1663 Liberty Drive
Bloomington, IN 47403
www.westbowpress.com
1 (866) 928-1240

ISBN: 978-1-5127-0297-2 (sc)
ISBN: 978-1-5127-0298-9 (e)

Library of Congress Control Number: 2015911935

Print information available on the last page.

WestBow Press rev. date: 07/31/2015

Contents

Preface

America has definitely changed since its birth. Then a very few men sat around tables, hammering out laws on how to be free and keep people safe in an uncertain world. Today thousands of politicians and judges are trying to define America in their own way. Many people have their own point of view and definite ideas on how America should function, which are heard only by family and friends, and perhaps co-workers. The only public voice heard by government is the people's vote. Although they seem to choose their representatives in the government, once in office, those elected officials enter a battle in judgment that is often won by a minority of people influencing them into making questionable decisions.

As Christians, do we follow the Golden Rule? Do we teach our children the difference between morality and immorality? Do they know what it really means to discriminate against another person? We can drift away from patriotic feelings very easily and take for granted the freedom that this country has offered for more than 230 years. Freedom takes work and nurturing—and in some cases, an ultimate sacrifice, a human life.

Chapter 1

America, Hello!

We are always reminded of how great the United States is and how appreciative we should be to live in a free country such as this. Our songs remind us that we live in "the land of the free and the home of the brave" and that "this land is your land; this land is my land." We sing, "God Bless America," and "My Country, 'Tis of Thee." And, yes, we should never take for granted this country—for it was bought and paid for by precious lives, all for the sake of freedom.

But I can't seem to shake a sense of insecurity, the feeling that our freedom is waning. These days, our government seems to be going backward in its ability to preserve the freedom and security in this country. Living in the United States is still better than living in any other country in the world. While this is true, why be satisfied with just some freedoms and opportunities and not demand both security and protection without interference from our government, knowing that the United States will *always* be the best place to live in the world?

In my opinion, if the country keeps going in the direction it is headed right now, this will not be the best place to live on the planet. In fact, it could be the most dangerous. It's a well-known fact that there are foreign countries at this moment that hate the United States. They cannot understand or comprehend the concept of a free world. And they dare to say that it's all in the name of religion.

Europe is known for that. Now didn't we break away from Europe and create our own United States? Why are we going back to other countries' traditions? Why can't we be the example for other countries to follow?

We have a unique government in our country today, and I must admit that I am not involved as much as perhaps I should be. But that's where trust comes in. I chose a lifestyle of raising a family and working what most would say is a regular job. The closest I would get to any government process or activity would be to vote or serve on a jury. So I have to rely on other people who have a true calling to serve other Americans and who will represent them in government issues with ethical and moral values.

As an automotive technician, years ago I used what was called *standard tools*. Everything was in fractions and inches. Then, for some reason (and to this day I don't know why), the automotive manufacturers started using metric-sized bolts and nuts. I didn't like the change, but to remain in the automotive field, I had to comply and buy the necessary tools. The metric system has been around for a long time but mostly in foreign countries. Now we have colors in our money. Do you see a trend here?

I recently read the Declaration of Independence for the first time in at least forty-five years. It's a shame that I wasn't more interested in history when I was a student. History back two hundred or even two thousand years ago is just fascinating.

While reading some of the things said by our forefathers—and knowing what is happening today and what happened over 230 years ago when our freedom was being established—I was a little taken back. Did we forget what a tyrant is? Almost on a daily basis, I wonder what is going to happen in the United States or even in my own city. For those of you who may not have read the Declaration in a long time—or maybe never—it is pretty clear that their king was doing things that people at that time thought were atrocities. These facts that the representatives wrote in the Declaration are eerily resonant with what is happening today.

Through the years, individuals in our government make subtle changes that may seem good, but they are actually making changes as a way to elevate themselves to a higher power in government—and ultimately to gain control over people. History has shown that humankind has been interested in its own power for thousands of years. From the kings and rulers of early Old Testament times to the modern-day Hitlers of the world, they create havoc and tremendous loss of human life.

This brings me to the point of my Christian view that humankind was created by God, yet we turned from God thinking we could do things on our own—and then failed miserably. Individuals need to recognize that without God being the main focus of their lives, they cannot live in the freedom and blessings God supplies. A person's very existence depends on allowing that inner person to guide his or her very steps in every facet of life.

Our forefathers recognized the need for a higher being's power to guide them. They understood and believed that there is good and evil in this world. Their writings were proof they were never ashamed to speak out about their beliefs in God. As it is today, the written word is a powerful tool—and they were not afraid to put down in words how important it was to trust in God for direction in governing a people. How sad it is that today our schools do not teach the uncompromised history of what our Founding Fathers really wanted the country to live by and the letters they wrote.

I read an article ʰfrom one of our Founding Fathers that led me to believe that unless our government officials speak truthfully and honestly, they will not be able to turn a wrong into a right.

Public officials and politicians today are destroying this country because they are not standing up to the most common truths and moral attitudes. Instead of singing psalms for one day on the steps of a building in Washington DC after we are attacked by terrorists, our representatives should be in prayer every morning, asking God to give them direction in leading this great nation that God gave us.

I had a friend who lost his wife of fifty-plus years, and he could never get over it. He just couldn't see why good people die and bad people live. He had always worked hard, helped other people, and tried to make a difference. When the news came on the TV or radio, he would get very upset about what he heard. In the last fifty years, he saw a change in America that was beyond his thinking. How could the American government take so much from the people and not give anything in return? Can the government really take our house and build a highway? Can the government take away our protection and claim we are safe, only to undermine our national security and be vulnerable to terrorists?

How is it possible to live in a free country, be successful and prosperous, and work all your life, only to find that your money is gone and the government that is supposed to protect you is not to be found? The very country he fought for is more interested in funding the murder of innocent babies than in protecting its citizens. It's no wonder my friend's heart failed him, and he is no longer with us. It was hard for him to grasp what was going on. When your own government puts fear in you (the IRS, for example), how can you live in peace?

This country has been through many ups and downs, particularly in our economy. This is nothing new. But it seems to always have a negative effect on other standards that we have to deal with. We always have to guard freedom—and sometimes fight for. When things don't go well at home, that weakens our ability to protect our country and the freedom it offers. The economy can always take care of itself if allowed to, provided capitalism is a very big part of that.

Think about this. Have you ever worked for someone who was broke or had no money? It doesn't matter if your employer is an individual, a family-operated business, or a big corporation. Someone had to have a vision of being successful, working hard, and meeting their needs and wants. Most people who want to come to America want to because they can have an opportunity to lift a family out of poverty and into a good life. If capitalism is restrained, it puts more power in the government and less desire in the people to achieve their dreams and goals in life; in short, it threatens their desire to succeed.

The United States government is not a person. You cannot call it, you cannot send it a letter, and you cannot e-mail it. At the end of a call, letter, or e-mail is a real, live person working in a position to serve their neighbors and country. The government is not a corporation. It is not a proprietorship. It has no business getting involved in business. Obviously, our leaders have no experience because they cannot even balance the country's budget. Pursuing foolish ends like going into the automobile and solar business and continuing to divert money to foreign soil when our own country is in crisis are evidence of ignorance gone to seed.

After reading some writings in history, I see that our economy is something we should build with honesty and character. Allowing it to be consumed with debt is a very dangerous tendency that must be dealt with harshly. This economy has been going pretty well for over two hundred years. Our economy has made us a very strong nation. The way it's going now, I don't think we'll last another twenty years before we go bankrupt and have to be subordinate to some undesirable people or countries. We have to stand up to the liberal thinking in this country.

Now, you Christians, don't get into a tizzy about America needing to help other countries. Yes, we are to go into the entire world and preach the gospel to everyone. Where do you think this money comes from? It certainly doesn't come from the liberals or our government. (The government does not have money. Not a penny. Zilch, nada.)The government gets its money from the people. As I see it, the government is funded by the people to support a military created to protect the United States from foreign enemies. The government is not supposed to feed the hungry or help the elderly. That's the churches' job. The church (people are the church, not a building) is designed to receive the monies so that they can establish the convent with God. When you don't give, that opens the door for someone else to come in and give with the understanding that you owe them.

When you are in debt up to your eyeballs, you are under bondage. And right now the United States is under so much bondage that it cannot tell right from wrong. I am no economic expert or business student, but my teachers taught me very basic common sense; for instance, if you have thirteen dollars in the bank, you cannot write a check for more than that. How can our elected officials have so much intelligence (and I use that term loosely) and still not understand this basic common sense?

Without doubt, this current administration and its supporters are leading our country right into socialism. You cannot divide the wealth in any country and expect it to survive. I have heard someone's opinion, "If you divide up all the money in the United States, within two years, the wealthy will have it back and the poor will have lost what they had." I have to agree with that statement. It's a fact that there are ambitious people, and there are lazy people. There are entrepreneurs—people who just plain work hard to excel and make themselves a better life—and there are people who just don't care and want to live off the government and handouts from other people.

I can't help but laugh when I see an advertisement by the government to help you get an education. They say, Get an education so you can get a good job and better yourself—perhaps even start your own business. Then the government comes in and taxes you beyond what is fair because you make too much money. It's the same liberal thinking these days that tells a child it's okay if you fail. You won't be penalized. Later in life you can get paid at your job (if you work instead of living off the government) the same as someone who went through eight years of college, because of some equality excuse. What's the sense in going to school if you are telling them it's okay if you don't pass? Where's the encouragement to keep the successful people working harder to fulfill their dreams?

People will not work hard if they have to give it to people who will not lift a finger for themselves. Why should they?

Chapter 2

Morality

I think Americans know what is moral and immoral. It's innate in the very fabric of human life. There's that little voice inside, telling you this is right or that is wrong. Most people would feel good about getting up in the morning and heading off to work with a couple of waves from neighbors and not even thinking about locking the front door. But that gives an opportunity for someone with an evil heart to disregard the property or well-being of others, whether that is an inner desire or something taught.

Good and moral life always produces harmony and love, so one cannot love and hate at the same time. Selfishness never considers other people's thoughts or feelings, so consequently there will always be discord and dissension.

Moral decay is nothing new on the earth. It's been around for thousands of years. But if you look at history, you will find it is always punished. No matter what religion you adhere to, if any, you may know about the cities of Sodom and Gomorrah mentioned in the Bible. They were totally consumed with immoral people, and rape, murder, and homosexuality were part of daily life. God wanted to destroy it, but a God-loving man named Abraham, didn't want him to because he thought he would destroy good people too. Abraham had a relative living there also. Well, as the story goes, the city was destroyed because there were no good, moral people living there save Abraham's relative, Lot. God led Lot and his family out just before the destruction came.

Through the ages, many evil cities and empires have been destroyed—the fall of Rome, the Dark Ages, on and on. Unfortunately, I feel we live in another era of evil and moral issues that are not being confronted, due to spiritual guidance not being allowed to deal with these issues surrounding us today.

I feel a plague of moral decay in the twentieth century started to gain its momentum in that very dark and evil year of 1973 (*Roe v. Wade*) when a court of supreme judges decided to become an *accessory* to murder of unborn children. At that moment, the law made murder legal to the person wanting to abort an unborn child and legalized being an accessory to this act. Now I ask you this, how can a country try to keep any kind of order, whether social or moral, if it cannot even protect the very beginning of a human life?

Is a spotted owl so much more important than an unborn child, that they stop roads, railways, and any progress at any cost to protect it? Is there no moral fiber left in our judges these days? For that matter, is there no accountability for our leaders to lead a moral life away from adultery, criminal activity, and sex acts? I believe there was a time when a court decision permitting the killing of unborn babies would have occasioned the ousting of a judge.

So did our forefathers think they would have to put in our constitution that unborn babies had a right to life? I think that was the furthest thought from their mind. They were fighting for their own lives and the freedoms of generations thereafter. They didn't have to try to decide whether life begins at conception or at the first cry after birth. Life was so precious at that time, they were willing to die so that others might enjoy freedom.

Those judges are ethically and morally responsible to guide us and protect us. In this case, however, they did not judge according to the will and good of the people. They decided based on the relentless pressure of a very few people. And if they say they were not influenced by others, they are guilty of not reaching down within themselves and searching for the right decision. Besides, you have to do what is good for society, not necessarily what a few people want. In the same way, you can't release a crazy person into society, especially when they have hurt themselves or someone else. There is a responsibility to deal with people who are not able to think or do for themselves.

I often hear the question, "What about a woman who was raped?" You could probably ask fifty Christians that same question, and some will say abortion is acceptable in those situations. I say, why not put your foot on evil's head and crush it? Look deep inside, see a life that was started by something so wrong and humiliating, and turn it into good. Thousands of people every day want to adopt babies. A person so traumatized by that evil act should try to overcome the hate that naturally flows from such a crime and instead consider giving an innocent life a chance to replace the evil with good.

I can't help but reflect on how a person, or a society for that matter, can get so upset when an eighteen-year-old man has sex with a consenting fifteen-year-old girl (out of wedlock) and they want to send him away for life. I even think you can go to jail for three to five years for cruelty to animals. Do you see where I am going here? Our society has determined the age when you are an adult and when you are not. Some of these things are wrong and should not be condoned. But when you don't put a value on a human life, these things are only around the corner of becoming an acceptable way of life allowed by a consenting society.

Do you know that if enough people sign a petition and rally to vote and create a law stating that their actions are a way of life, society would have to accept it? God forbid that enough people might allow that to happen. But just look at how many people support the pro-choice movement.

You think that could never happen? Forty years ago I would never have dreamed that people would change the law from a marriage being between a man and a woman to a union between a man and another man or between two women. When I was growing up, I thought coming out of the closet meant coming out of the closet. You go in, you get what you need, and you come out. You go in to play hide-and-seek, they find you, and you come out. Had I known then what I know now, I would never have opened the door. (Just a little humor.)

Okay, I hear the gears turning. You already think that I am hateful to gay people, but quite the opposite is true. In my Bible it says to love your neighbor as yourself. If I hated my neighbors because they were gay but loved my neighbors because they went to my church and believed the way I do, that would be hypocritical. Not to mention how disappointed God himself would be in me. According to my Bible, homosexuality is sin. I did not write the laws of nature, nor did I instill in humankind a certain moral mentality. That was God's doing. And because I believe he is the creator of man and the universe, I dare not argue with him. Although I do many times, I lose, and he lets me get away with it.

Jesus never hated anyone. In fact his love for us was so deep that we could not fathom his dying the way he did for us. And all he wanted was for us to just believe in him and trust him that his sole purpose was to save humankind from the certainty of eternal death. But be very aware he never condoned sin. He knew the evil spirit that drove people to the sinful nature and had to address that by confronting the very people he loved.

When he met up with a woman who was accused of being an adulteress, he did not snub her or curse her. He first asked the very people who were accusing her whether they were without sin. They had no answer for Jesus. Perhaps some of them were living in sin themselves, and then recanted on condemning her. But Jesus had a statement for the woman. "Neither do I condemn thee: go, and sin no more" (John 8:11, KJV). He didn't give her a license to commit adultery. He made it very clear that it was sin. So if a Christian disagrees with a gay lifestyle, it's the sin, not the person, that is hated. Granted, many Christians forget that, don't practice the love part, and create a sense of hatred of the person. Jesus was never tolerant of sin. He addressed it in no uncertain terms. And so should the Christian.

Chapter 3

Patriotism

As I write this chapter, I read a story about a high school in Colorado that will not allow students to have a sprit week honoring America. As I understand it, spirit week is a time when the students have a chance to do something that makes school fun and exciting. It also gives the students an opportunity to show a little creativity for whatever the theme happens to be. It might be who can dress the craziest by wearing their clothes inside out or who has the wildest hairdo.

In this case, it would be about celebrating America. Yes that's what I said: Celebrating America. Are You Kidding Me, Colorado? I CAN'T YELL IT MUCH LOUDER ON PAPER. I am fast losing respect for that state. (You forty-nine other states are in the same boat. I will get to my next rant about that state farther on in the book.)

So some administrator says that they don't want to offend visitors or immigrants from other countries. They don't want to make anyone feel uncomfortable. Hogwash. I am so offended and uncomfortable right now that I want to break my keyboard. I just hope and pray that a soldier in Afghanistan, an American in harm's way, every minute of every day, serving to protect us, doesn't read that article, knowing that some school administrator doesn't give a hoot about America.

Is this administrator even an American? I think not! It appalls me to think this person would not stand up for America here on free soil. What courage and selflessness our servicemen and women have, putting their lives in danger while I sit here and write and also while these kids have an opportunity to be in a classroom under the freedom of America, to learn and get an education and have a great future. Millions of children all over the world don't even have food to eat, let alone the opportunity to obtain an education.

By the way, the students and parents who were told that they could not have this celebration were asked to remain anonymous. The parents were afraid that their children would face reprisals from liberal educators. America, if you don't get a hold of this nonsense and anti-America mentality, especially in the school system, there will be no more America.

What does patriotism mean these days? The word is heard quite often in recent years. As I understand it, patriots have a love, respect, and pride toward their country. They will fight for the right to be free.

That's a pretty straightforward meaning, so I will go with that. Do you love your country? Are you in agreement with the way it was founded? Does the thought of freedom make you and your family feel secure? I would hope to think that you are very agreeable with the way our country was established. Now I ask you, if you were born here, did you receive enough knowledge and education about our country to believe that America is the best place to live in the world?

Did you come from another country because you heard that the United States was a better place to live, with better opportunities to succeed and the chance to feel safe and secure? What I don't understand are the people who come to our country to improve themselves and get a chance to give their families a better way of life then mock the very country that gave them that new life and want to change it to what they just left. People's heritage is a proud thing, and they should know about who they are and where they came from. America is an exceptional country to be able to show and tell all the different cultures from around the world. But the American way of life needs to be at the forefront and remain the foundation of liberty and freedom.

It is commonplace in my state for buildings to be painted all the same color—the color of another country, with signs in their own language that I can't understand. I find instructions on an item I purchased where I have to find the page with the English version so I can use the product. There are also the phone calls I make having to listen to a different language to get to my call. Yes, this sounds like I'm a little angry, but it's more frustration than anything else. I'll admit, sometimes my angry button gets pushed, but I don't think it's without merit.

I try to imagine sometimes what our forefathers would say if someone told them when they wrote our constitution, "Now be sure and write this in English, Spanish, French, and a few other languages." I think old Ben Franklin would have taken off his glasses, rubbed them a little with his cleaning cloth, put them back on, and said, "I beg your pardon."

John F. Kennedy said (my paraphrase), "Don't ask your country to keep giving you a handout. Ask if you can serve your country by voting good and honest people into office. Offer to serve in the military or help our vets." I think he was trying to tell us to build up our country to be stronger and safer, not change it according to behavior and traditions from outside our borders.

I would highly encourage you to read John F. Kennedy's inaugural address on January 20, 1961. Democrat or Republican, this man had an awareness of the almighty God and how we need to rely on that inner strength in our daily lives. A lot of liberals have gotten far away from the ideals and qualities of John Kennedy and have elevated their own agenda to empower themselves.

Have we not learned from history what to do and not to do? What better teacher than an opportunity to learn from the past? We can only predict or assume certain results in the future by our actions in the present, but we can expect a positive result in the future by knowing the outcome of the past.

I refer a lot to our forefathers for what this country should be and aspire to, but there are many, many other Americans, even in the last sixty to seventy years, who know what it takes to keep America strong, safe, and great. Can we be forefathers to our descendants and be an example of what it takes to keep a country strong and thriving in the midst of hard times and struggles against unhealthy change and tolerant attitudes? God help us.

Chapter 4

Right and Wrong

What is right and what is wrong? Are they one and the same? Is it just what society says it is? Who decides what is legal and what is illegal? What is moral and what is immoral?

There is and will always be a direction for humanity But one has to first believe in God our creator to have a spiritual sense of what that direction is and to determine what is right and moral and what is wrong and immoral.

Changing something in society from illegal to legal doesn't make it moral. Morals start from the heart. Moral issues are generally understood by most people who have a sense of proper behavior. But like anything good, these attitudes can be corrupted and sometimes made to be an acceptable way of life.

There are about eighty words in the dictionary related to the word *immoral*. In true Christian belief, the only truth about what is right and wrong comes from the heart of man, influenced by the very spirit and nature of God. If we loved God and our neighbor with all our heart, there would not be the conflicts and hatred we have today. To not embrace this concept will have ill effects in all aspects of human life.

In biblical writings the consequences of independently declaring what is right and what is wrong are clear.

> Woe to those who call evil good, and good evil;
>
> Who put darkness for light, and light for darkness;
>
> Who put bitter for sweet, and sweet for bitter! (Isaiah 5:20, KJV)

Since the fall of humanity from the grace of God, people have been trying to decide right and wrong for themselves. We do not have the ability to know the best way to live life. We cannot see the future to determine the outcome of certain behavior. We cannot create anything, so we do not have the ability to manage anything on our own. Anything we do without God, acknowledging only ourselves, is vain and unproductive, leading only to our own demise.

People talk about nature, or Mother Nature. I think the term is used rather loosely. Isn't it a created surrounding on the planet Earth? Are there not certain laws that come into play that make up the earth?

Even if you are not a Christian believer, science itself can tell you about certain laws that cannot be broken or altered; if they are, dramatic phenomena can happen. If you incorrectly mix certain chemicals, catastrophic results can occur. Now if you mix two parts of hydrogen with one part oxygen, you get water, which is a good thing or the right thing to do, unlike the former which would be a bad thing or the wrong thing to do.

So who decides what is right and what is wrong? There are obviously too many *different* people in this world, some seven billion, to rely on one making all the right and wrong judgments and decisions. I believe only God can do that job. So what do we do in the meantime? Do we shake it off as most people do?

Do we just try to survive and go with the flow as best as we can? Do we even care so long as our personal space is not affected, with nobody cramping our style? Can conflict on these issues of who is right and who is wrong stay objective without irreversible results or consequences? Perhaps the answer is yes and no.

Christians are supposed to portray the attributes of love and forgiveness. Good people all over the globe will have differences of opinion as to what is right and wrong, but can we operate our lives almost daily on a case-by-case basis to determine the severity of the disagreement and to decide the action to take, whether to brush it off as one's rightful opinion or to stand up and fight for the cause?

Chapter 5

Discrimination

I n the biblical writings of Solomon, he states, "There is nothing new under the sun," and discrimination is not new.

What does the word *discrimination* really mean? Is it a physical action? Is it something that can be touched? Or is a state of mind? We know that if a person or persons react differently toward other people because of their skin color or their ethnic background, we would say they are expressing discrimination. We also know that those who can look at a piece of art, for instance, and know the difference between the real thing and a copy are able to discriminate between good and bad. And finally, being able to recognize that things are different doesn't mean that they are bad; nor is the ability a bad thing.

Now it appears in the first definition that this is a physical action taking place. For example; a group of boys, that like to hang out on the corner wearing Levis and white T-shirts with their baseball caps on sideways will hassle a group of boys wearing nice clothes and combed hair going down the same street to the ice cream store. They don't like the way they look or present themselves, so they pick on them. And there is a good chance the groups won't hang out together.

In the second definition, this focuses on the inner person. In the same example, a boy from the first group has been friends with a boy from the second group. For some reason the first boy has a desire to associate with the first group of boys, but because of his friendship with the other boy, and knowing his good qualities and attributes, he makes sure the other is not harmed in any way. He tells his friends, "Hey, this guy is cool; leave him alone."

This is where the third definition comes in.

The first boy has the ability to recognize the differences between them, but that is not a factor in their friendship. But what if perhaps the first boy has constantly berated people who dress nicely with their hair combed and said that they were always treating him badly because of the way *he* dressed? Because the second boy hung out with these people that berated the first boy, but did not share the objectionable clothing by the others, he also will be labeled as discriminatory simply by association.

I realize that the word *discrimination* has many meanings, but the area I want to address has to do with people and their inner self. To discriminate between right and wrong, between moral and immoral, seems to be quite the issue these days.

When I was growing up, I didn't really pay any attention to discriminatory things. I was raised to never hate anyone. In fact, I was not even allowed to say the word *hate*. The main issue in this country when I was a youth was whites against blacks and blacks against whites. I wasn't really exposed to it, so it didn't really affect me. I could not imagine telling another person that they could not drink out of the same water fountain that I did because of their color. I didn't know any better. I was raised with the outlook that some people are white, some are black, some are red, and some just look different. But they were still people like me. I never could understand how people would refer to blacks as a different race of people. My understanding is that we are all of one race, the human race.

This sprang from my belief in the creation by God, who made humanity out of the earth. Scientists can tell you that the dirt has many colors. If you have ever seen the Grand Canyon or Sedona in Arizona, you know how beautiful it can be. To see that red rock of Sedona glowing in the evening or the many colors of sand and stone in the Grand Canyon is breathtaking. Well, God saw it good to create people in different colors and looks. Can you imagine all people looking alike? What if all flowers were the same color, with green petals, green stalks, and no other color? That just would not be pleasant to the eye.

Now here in the Arizona desert, anything green looks good. (In case you didn't get that, I was just attempting a joke.) Here in the desert it's real brown due to not much rain and so much hot sun. So anything that gets green, mainly in the fall and spring, is a welcome sight. Part of the fallible inner self of humans is that we cannot properly discern the existence and purpose of humankind and God's purpose for us. Now we look through glasses that are cloudy and don't see what is truly out there.

As I said earlier, almost every day, headline news in this country is ripping the very fabric of our freedom. Today is no exception. In California, a Christian family enterprise was put out of business because of their beliefs. It's another case of nonbelievers accusing Christians of discrimination because they will not accept or condone what their Christian belief condemns. In Arizona a short time later, they wanted to pass a law that gave Christians the right to refuse service to anyone or produce anything that goes against their beliefs. This bill was meant to sustain the right to religious belief. This bill being vetoed is a clear sign of discrimination toward the Christians, speaking for those not favoring a law to protect Christians, saying to them instead, "You have no rights based on what you believe."

Discrimination comes from the heart. If you are taught discrimination from childhood, you will grow to have that attitude. We cannot allow this to grow in our children and expect to drive it out of them in adulthood. This quote from Thomas Jefferson points out that "bigotry is the disease of ignorance, of morbid minds"—in other words, it is a mental disorder, not a natural-born instinct: Education from birth drives away this mentality. We see children all the time who play with other children from all walks of life without animosity or hatred because to them they are just other little people.

When there was a push for a Martin Luther King Day in Arizona and many people opposed it (including myself), many accused us of being racist. Well, that made my blood boil. Some of my dear friends are black, and I took that very personally. This was not a race issue. The more the race card gets used, the angrier I get. And yes, it's put me into a discrimination attitude. Some people make you that way just to prove there point. What people fail to see is this is clearly a reverse discrimination they are producing that is much worse than what went before.

Granted, people can make you discriminate because of their foolish talk or actions, but that should not cloud your judgment because of just a few people. It is the Christian's job to always act out of love and not hate. Retaliation such as others practice is not the Christian way. This is where the Christian life stands out in love rather than hate. However, we should always stand up for what we think is right and moral.

Chapter 6

Education

Training a child is one big job if you take it seriously. The responsibility lies on you to educate your children so they grow up knowing how to feed and take care of themselves and live a healthy and stress-free life as much as possible. We always want our children to realize their dreams and live a better life than we did. When children slip through the cracks of proper training, they become disillusioned about what is right and proper and what is wrong and misleading. If a parent disciplines a child *without love*, the child grows up to resent the parent and the punishments. The child's attitude becomes "When I have children, I am not going to spank them or make them be home at 9 o'clock. I am going to be their friend. I am going to let them have their own life without restrictions."

When you plant a small tree, you cannot just stick it in the ground and throw dirt and some water on it. The tree does not know how to stand up straight and reach for the warmth of the sun and its nutritional rays. There is no foundation to keep it up. So you put strong and firm support stakes in the ground to keep the tree growing in the right direction until it can build its own foundation and stand on its own.

So now we have rebellious children growing up and taking positions in government, changing the strong foundations built by those who had not only common sense but also the fortitude to know what is best for the people. Just look at the new laws that are being passed every day. For example; years ago, marijuana was considered to be a drug, a mind-altering substance that should not be taken. The people who believe in open-mindedness and tolerance always want to take the easy way out. "Let's not discipline; let's educate." Okay, so where was the education? Did we learn in school how the effects of drugs can harm people? Was it driven into our minds that this destroys families and friends? No.

Now we have these same people changing the way we look at things that were considered wrong and allowing them to work their way into society, benefiting only the government, funneling more money and more power to the people in office. Yes, many medical drugs have saved countless millions of lives. And these medications have been a godsend to people who need them. However, there is still no excuse for allowing these to be used in a manner that is destroying our society.

How can a country as great as this one be so ignorant of the future when they have the past to learn by? Look at what alcohol has done in this country—the breaking up of families, the alcohol-related deaths, and let us not overlook the medical issues. Was the fight against it too much, so the easy way out was chosen instead? What drugs will be tolerated next just to avoid a protest of the few?

History does and will repeat itself. When people walk in an evil path, they will be overtaken with evil. How far back will we be taken this time? Will we be able to recover? Will even this generation live to see uprightness in society that will lead them to a more purposeful and successful life? Will spirituality once again become the norm?

As a Christian, I have to believe in certain spiritual truths. There is a spiritual realm that surrounds the earth, and it is very real. If you do not believe that, then it is very difficult to interpret what is happening on this earth and why things are the way they are. There is good and there is evil. Most people think they know the difference, but many times a false "truth" gets in the way. Cataracts develop over the eyes of one's inner self, and people by the millions are unable to see clearly.

> *For without the belief of a Providence* [God conceived as the power sustaining and guiding human destiny], *that takes cognizance of, guards, and guides, and may favor particular persons, there is no motive to worship a Deity, to fear his displeasure, or to pray for his protection.*
>
> —Benjamin Franklin

You can't prove there is no God. Nor can I prove that there *is* one. It takes faith. All we have to do is look into the sky at a billion stars, and if we don't realize that there is a Creator, we are foolish and twisted within ourselves, with no real understanding or purpose in life.

Chapter 7

Christian Bashing

If men are so wicked with religion, what would they be if without it?

—Benjamin Franklin

B eing brought up in a Christian home, I learned very young about God, Jesus, and the writings in the Bible. I accepted the teachings about Christ because I believed in my parents. As I grew in the things of the church and gained a deeper understanding of God, I made my own decisions about the faith and chose to believe the teachings in the Bible were true.

Living in a free country never gave me a sense of fear that would result in believing in the Christian religion. (Religion itself is very misleading and hypocritical. Religion is what put Jesus on the cross. But this is for a different book.) I believed in our government to protect me in my beliefs because it was in our Constitution, which was backed up by the most powerful military in the world, and the chance of anything changing never crossed my mind. That is, until now.

I was taught that in many countries, Christians were not allowed to pray or go to church for fear of their lives. It's pretty hard to grasp that kind of living when you live in a society that practically has a church on every corner. Some people in my generation and a little earlier tried to convince Americans that God was dead. Where did they come up with that? Why did they come up with that? They can't prove that any more than I can prove that he is alive. After all, believing in something you can't see is called faith. You can't see me loving you. You have to take my word for it. I can show you things that express my love, but you also have to have a deeper understanding to decide whether it is genuine. In biblical times, it didn't matter if you believed in any type of religion; if you didn't comply with the way the particular government believed, you could be killed.

In America today, I feel that our very freedom to worship and believe the way we desire is being compromised every day. Christians and Christian groups are being singled out every day.

Earlier I talked about a family who were driven out of business because of their Christian beliefs. They were asked to perform a service for someone that contradicted the very core of their Christian faith. They were ridiculed and mocked for it and ultimately lost their business because of it. I truly believe that if this was a Muslim business and *they* refused to perform this service, not much at all would have been said. In fact, if anything was said, the whole Muslim world would condemn it and, as we've seen, cause deadly attacks from radicals because of it, all in the name of religion. Non-Christians have become so intolerant of Christians and tolerant of other faiths that it is a clear sign of Christian persecution in America today.

Chapter 8

A Nation of Strength?

I n order for a nation to be born, it must first have the desire to be free. It must be able to grow and sustain itself. Its mentality must be that it can survive no matter what goes on around it. Through history, nations built on slavery and torment of other people never survived because most people will always have a desire to live in freedom. The evil people who desire to dictate and suppress other people so they can have power and control can never endure.

There is a verse in the Bible that says: "And if a house be divided against itself, that house cannot stand" (Mark 3:25, KJV). That does not mean that if a person in a household disagrees with another person about how meals should be cooked or how the beds are to be made, that household will break apart. Although divorces have come from things more insignificant, the strength of a union is based on moral, ethical, and spiritual standards. Although many say that is nonsense, it will never change a universal law.

Spiritual beliefs are always the center of any human confrontation or differences. If there is more than one religious belief in one household, there will always be conflict.

The United States was given a gift from the country of France years ago, the Statue of Liberty. It reminds me of the time when King Solomon ruled in Israel, and people from other countries would brings gifts to him. They did this, I believe, out of respect for not only his widely known great wisdom but the power that Israel had at that time.

Groups of people call on great kings with gifts to show they are a peaceful people and avoid a possibility of attack from the more powerful nation. When France gave us that gift, I believe they were solidifying their alliance with us out of respect, knowing we were the more powerful country. Unfortunately, that is not the view of many countries about the United States.

If we are to become, once again, the more powerful and reputable country we once were and a beacon of generosity and compassion, we have to get back to a spiritual harmonious attitude. Our military must once again be priority in the eyes of every American. Allowing our flag to be burned in the name of personal expression slaps the face of every man and woman in uniform. I will never believe that the forefathers of this country would condone these actions.

Final Thoughts

I n just a few weeks since the writings earlier in this book, there have been some major changes and unsettling stories in the United States. As a Christian I can sometimes allow changes in this country to get a grip on my thinking and take it down a road I have no business being on. One of the most essential sayings in the Bible is "Fear not." I know what is at the beginning of that book, and I know how it ends. We win. But until the race is finished, I still have to run with patience and guidance from almighty God.

America may go on for many decades or perhaps centuries. It may not be the same as it was two centuries ago or even twenty years ago. Perhaps it will be the best it has ever been. But in my mind's eye, I see a change that would be unrecognizable to most Americans today. The United States, I feel, is on a road to collapse and hard times or perhaps a more destructive scenario.

The earth groans from the weight of sin and disobedience to God and is destined for more destruction unless people turn back to God and repent. Again, looking back into history, people failed to obey God, and the earth was destroyed—except for Noah and his family, because of his continued obedience to God. Although God promised to never destroy the earth again, rebellion against God resulted in people's destruction time and time again. When people believed God and obeyed his commandments, God would make them triumphant and heal their land. Such is the case with God's people, the Israelites, and anyone who believed in him.

Entities such as the entertainment industry must not dictate the way this country runs or influence the way people live unless it is toward a spiritual and godly way of life.

This is a case of learning from history. Why do we go down a road full of holes and dangerous cliffs, only to be riddled with poverty, despair, and failure? We have the answers. We have the tools to make things right. So why do we choose to think in a way that is known to be destructive?

America, the alarm is sounding, and many of you continue to push the snooze button. We have to wake up and get those trains going on the right tracks, or we will keep having collisions that will only get worse. Look around you and see the destruction that's happening: the earthquakes, the tsunamis, hurricanes, blizzards, droughts, tornadoes, and the list just goes on. We now have the return of viruses and flu's that have been gone for decades or even centuries. This is not just a coincidence. The deterioration of morals and our disobedience to God are causing this groaning in the earth. The devastation and destruction will continue. People around the world are dying in greater numbers and in horrifying ways. Not since Hitler have we had such needless destruction of human life, but we could be on a path that leads to the same devastation.

I feel that on September 11, 2001, God turned his back on America because he had to. America has been straying away from God, and the results are in. "Blessed is the nation whose God is the Lord" (Psalm 33:12, KJV). Curses stand over the nations in disobedience.

True Christians should never compromise or be tolerant when it comes to immoral or anti-Christian attitudes, but they also must understand and live out the commandment, *"Love the Lord your God with all your heart, soul, and mind, and love your neighbor as yourself."* That doesn't mean they are to be mean and nasty. A change has to come from the inside.

Christians must always recognize the driving force behind the evil of this world. A major issue today with society is the judgmental attitude that Christians display toward others, particularly people of a different faith. God is the ultimate judge. We are only to pray and share our beliefs with others, so that they might also be free not only in their physical life on this earth but also their spiritual life.

We are engaged in spiritual warfare every day. Our foe has already been defeated, and we must not carry this fight to the physical side of our being. God has given us the blessings and ability to live a good life on this earth if we follow his plan and not the foolishness of people's selfish thinking.

Endnote

i   Thomas Jefferson, The Library of Congress

Printed in the United States
By Bookmasters